The Indie Artist Struggle

Ladi Miz

Published by

Ladi Miz publishing

Printed by the United States of America

Book cover design: Ladi Miz publishing

Copyrights 2020 - by Ladi Miz

All rights reserved. No parts of this book may be reproduced or transmitted in any form or by any means without written permission from the author.

TABLE OF CONTENTS

Starting With The Basic	1
My History and Beginning Experience	6
What You Need	19
More of what you need to know	36
Know your codes and numbers	71

STARTING WITH THE BASIC

We all have dreams. Following your dreams is where the work comes in. Being able to live your purpose is most people's life goal. They say you only live once but that's not true. You live every day but you only die once. Being an independent artist in the year 2020 is the new wave. Being able to survive a pandemic and follow your dream is a blessing. In this book, we are going to talk about some of the things that you need to know when trying to be an independent artist. I will break down my thoughts and experiences to give you some helpful tips that can help you establish yourself as an artist that gets paid for their talent. But first, let's get past the ugly part. I'm not trying to portray negativity but I'm not going to sugar it either. You have to have tuff skin in this game.

So I am going to shoot it straight. In this industry, you learn very quickly that you do not have any friends. You'll also learn very quickly that not everyone will believe in you until you start to really make it. Sometimes, that will also include your family members. A lot of times, people seem to follow only what others do, meaning; if someone else says a song is hot, they'll take a listen. They are less likely to be the one to give you their opinion first. People normally like what is repetitively played over and over again. They become programmed by the programmers. A lot of people think they're making their own decisions when it comes to a certain style of music but they don't know that they are actually being programmed. We all fall victim to this, I know I have.

However, it does not mean that you really don't have a mind of your own and it does not mean that you don't know what type of genre of music you like; it simply means; whatever is popular, people tend to gravitate more towards it. A lot of independent artists get very frustrated especially at their early stage because they are expecting people to care about their passion and people just simply don't. I know it sounds mean but it's the case most but not all of the time. You may have a couple of people and maybe even someone who is willing to support you and invest in you but that is rare and you're lucky if you have that. Most people are only trying to take your money and see what they can get from you or even see if you can make them more money. There is no one out here really trying to make somebody else rich without making themselves rich. The game of music has changed over the years.

I can't speak on the level of being a mainstream artist. I can only speak from my experience. And from my experience in the short period of taking this music seriously and investing in it, I have learned a lot along the way. I have also learned from others who were willing to give me advice. However, no one really taught me just out of the blue. I was a customer of some sort to them. Meaning I was spending my money. So maybe that's why I got that information. Not saying that they would not have given it to me without me being a customer but I've never experienced that as of yet. So what I'm going to get into with you guys today is all of the things to look out for as an independent artist. I will give you some tips on how you can protect yourself and what you should be looking out for. I'm going to give you some tips on figuring out if this is really meant for you.

A lot of times people think that being an independent artist is easy. It is not, if you do not have the money and a team, you may actually need a label. But needing the label means you work for them and you need to understand that. You also need to understand that if you sign with the label, it means that this label is investing their money in your career. It further explains that you don't have the money to invest in your career so you have to give something up. What is that going to be? That's all up to you. Any and everything can be negotiated; you just can't be so quick to sign because something feeds your ego at the time. A lot of artists got jerked in this music industry because they were sold a dream. They were told they were going to be famous and everyone would know who they are. They want to hear millions of people scream their name and they want to feel like a superstar.

A lot of times, some people can offer you that but they'll get rich and you will be famous and broke. A lot of artists that you probably grew up listening to or listen to now may be in a situation like that. They may also be in a situation of a 360 deal. A 360 deal is a deal where everybody gets paid around you and you get paid last. In my opinion, it's not a good deal but to each his own. Once real money starts rolling in and an artist starts to see how much their talent is generating and a large amount of income is coming, they will soon realize that those types of deals are robbing them blind. There are some people in the industry that like to talk about how artists were robbed when they were the main ones out here robbing them. These people can't be trusted. Just brings me back to the fact that you have no friends in this game. It's always business and never personal. You have to do your own research, hire your old lawyers and separate your personal feelings from your business feelings.

MY HISTORY AND BEGINNING EXPERIENCE

Let me first give you a little bit of history about who I am and what I've done so far so that you can understand the experience I am going to talk to you about and the lessons that I learned. I want to make sure that you know so that you can either not make the same mistake I made or do what you think would actually work for you. So first, let's start with the very beginning. I started rapping at the age of 11. Listening to Dougie Fresh and Slick Rick one day and then I decided to write my own rhymes over top of theirs. I started to block those out theirs and say my own words and I loved every moment of it. It's just something that naturally came out of me. From there, I loved it and enjoyed it so much that I continued to write. I started looking for instrumentals so that I did not have to block out the artist's lyrics and with time I got better and better. In middle school, I was known to be one of the hottest female rappers.

I used to battle people, mainly guys. Most of my close friends were guys and we would hang out and record songs. I also performed for the first time at the age of 15 in Harlem at a place called Victoria 5 next to the Apollo. I had a manager at that time who saw potential in me. That relationship didn't end well once he tried to sleep with me. At this time, I was living in the house with him, his wife and kids. I was very close with his kids and wife so that was devastating to me because that relationship wasn't ever the same since then. That was my first experience of being in the industry having someone who showed interest in helping me and believing in me and my dream. Someone willing to help me get on. At the time, I didn't understand what a manager got out of it. I was just a young 15-year-old girl wandering the streets. But even worse, I guess my lifestyle made him think that I was easy and I would lie down with him and disrespect his wife and my friends and most of all myself but that didn't happen. I left and went next-door to a neighbor's house and told them what happened. I later told the wife and daughter. Then I left and moved out. At that time, I had public assistance and I was getting a rental income that was going directly to them so I could live there.

So, everyone was benefiting all across the board. I was living there having a place to stay but also being able to do what I want when I want and however I wanted to. I knew that I could go and come as I please and there would be no restrictions. They knew that me being on public assistance will also Bring in income plus I had food stamps so I didn't come empty-handed. I had a reputation of knowing how to rap so most people in my town knew that. I was introduced to someone that was from Queens, New York and they took me to Queens to meet a producer. My cousin and I went out to Queens and they wanted me to rap for the guy. I was very immature at the time and was dating one of the guys that brought me there. When I walked in, I saw a lot of platinum plaques all around the wall of some of my favorite artists that I listen to which were salt and pepper LL Cool J and a few others.

I was very scared and shy and did not want to rap. So they told the guy to bring me back next time when I felt more comfortable. They did not want to force it. I never went back. That may have been either a good or bad opportunity for me that I missed that day. That opportunity could have been good and ended up bad meaning I was young and dumb, knew nothing about the business and most likely, I could have got jerked and taken advantage of. A good opportunity that could've been my break into the music business early because I obviously was running into the right people that were dealing with people and helping people that were already in the industry. But the one thing that we have to remember is; you never really know what's going on behind the scenes. Although people may seem like they're winning and life is great, it may not really be the truth. A lot of artists are not really winning; they are just being put in positions to look like they are. There's always somebody behind the scenes that's really getting the money while the artist is getting crumbs. But I will get into what you should know later on to put an end to that.

A lot of artists did not know how to get the money that was owed to them; they just got the up-front money that was promised to them. This is why the independent wave is so big right now. Now some time has passed and I ended up meeting my daughter's father who was a DJ, rapper and producer. I Was about 16 or 17 years old. Being with him helped me stay off the streets and stay out of trouble and it gave me a place where I can do what I love. Being with him was fun and I no longer needed to run the streets. I had a place where I could record my songs and get the experience I needed in the studio. His basement was the spot where everybody went to in Nyack New York. He would allow many artists and DJs who are now even on these big radio stations to come record or mix at his house for nothing.

He was very smart and did a lot of reading. Back then, he had already created my performance rights organization account. He was trying to do all the right things for me as an artist. I knew nothing about the business at all. All I just wanted to do was write and rap. People knew who I was in town. I was local. I loved it and it fed my ego as a young girl. I thought that that was good enough back then. I knew that I wanted more. I just didn't know how I would get it. Like most people today. You would be surprised how many people actually do not know the business part of this industry. I'm not going to say I know everything because I don't. As I stated before, I can only tell you what I know and learned along the way. Back then when we were rapping in the basement and recording songs, they were getting registered with the performance rights organization which is great because that can be tracked and you get some credit if it ever went anywhere. But it was more to it than that. The good thing about me is that I was writing very early at the age of 11 so I didn't need a ghostwriter. Time went on and then I met other people in the industry, big-name people who work with big-name artists. I work with producers that gave me beats and mixed and mastered my songs. These producers were also teaching me things that I needed to know along the way.

I had the attitude at that time that if they knew mainstream artists and had connections, why weren't they helping me get on. But I quickly learned that if there was nothing in it for someone else they are not going to help you. And also, you should have the material that they think will get you and them to the next level. If they really believe in something, then maybe they may try to see who can help you but a lot of times, some of these people can't help you either. The point is; you have to help yourself. Doing the music on and off became the norm for me. Recording, having fun with it, playing it for me and my friends but never doing anything with it and just letting it sit where it is or sitting on the CD. I knew nothing about promotion and marketing. Promotion for me was letting my friends hear it.

The time I decided I was going to get out there to get noticed and invest in myself, I got pregnant. Things were put on pause and like many of us; we go through our ups and downs which can slow the process up as well. That's not an excuse, it's just life. But for me, it was more important to focus on my child and kids than anything else. Rule number one; family is always first. And when I say family I mean immediate in your household. Not the ones who want to come around when they think there's something in it for them. You can always tell who they are by looking at your past; who was there when you had nobody? If they don't know your story, how can they say they knew and were a part of your struggle? If you have to find out what I went through by reading my book and you are my family then you obviously were absent in my struggles. I learned the hard way with my own experience and a lot of people who I thought cared about me eventually showed me they never really did. Even the people I cared deeply for exposed their true colors. When I became unusable, I became disposable. Eventually, I got to a point where I was no longer doing music and it wasn't even a thought. Things started to change, my love for it started to decrease. I did not pay attention to what was happening in the industry and noticed it was very different, the sound changed. I didn't like any of it and I saw people stressing and losing so much money. I'm so happy that I walked away from doing music. I had so much more money that I was able to invest in a property and other stuff that I wanted.

While I sat back and watched everybody still chasing a dream getting broker and broker, I was stress-free stacking paper. However, I felt like something was missing and I wasn't 100% happy because I wasn't doing what I love. I even tried helping family members and ended up getting disrespected and used in the end. In the process, I was learning from other people's mistakes. Their ego was their downfall and was holding them back. Plus some people will swear you are using them when they don't even have shit. One thing to remember is; your ego can be your downfall. Millions are doing what you do, so to most people, you aren't that special and if you are, you have to prove it. You have to be careful who you have around you. Even in our families, some people are very jealous. Their energy can destroy everything around you. I learned that the hard way. Anyway, to fast forward the turn of events, one day I got a phone call from someone asking me to get back into the music industry.

It didn't take much to convince me because that was the piece I thought I was missing. It definitely was a gas up moment because I later found out that it wasn't because the person cared about me and my dreams or talent. I thought they wanted to see me succeed and even really truly believed in me but it was more for their benefit and their company and what they were trying to accomplish as a label with having an artist on their label. Now, don't get me wrong I appreciate the call but it wasn't really for my benefit. So basically, if there was no purpose for them, I would have never received that call and they would have never cared. I decided to get back into the music and when I did, I started to move in such a way that was an old-school way of thinking. The industry has changed so much and it's been over 12 years. The sound has even changed. I was also used to being able to have your own sound but having your own sound isn't in anymore. The game changed and people only liked you if you sound like someone else. Trap music was in now. Being different was no longer respected. Now you need to actually sound like someone that was out and now everyone sounds the same. I was trying to have an open mind but it was a bit of a struggle to get this new wave. People that knew the game in this reinvented industry could clearly tell that I didn't know and was taken advantage of.

I was overcharged and played by many people white and black. A Lot of times, we as black people like to say things like we can't even trust our own people. Well, it doesn't matter what color you are, if they are grimy, that's just what it is. I also noticed my sound was considered to now be a school sound and at first, I used to take offense to that. Now I accept it with pride. My job is not to fit in with kids and my target audience will respect and understand my sound. Not saying that people should not evolve but you should always remain true to yourself and keep your sound. You can switch up your flow a bit but you should always remain who you are because that's not something you have to try to do because that comes naturally.

So 2018 was when I made a decision that I want to try this music industry stuff for real. Since then, I've put out three albums, started my own podcast and I've been working on building my brand. I wrote a book telling my life story about me growing up. I'm not the most popular person in the world, but people know who I am and it all came from footwork and me grinding. I would host on other people's stations which gave me the experience of dealing with and talking to an audience. I host an independent radio station on DJC Radio global and I also have my old podcast called From Da Ground Up. I started learning what it was like to be on the other side. This exposed me to new experiences in the entertainment industry. It also made it easier for me to connect and build a relationship with other artists.

This became a way to connect with other artists without automatic beef attached to it. I'm sure you are wondering why and how? Well because they no longer see you as a competition but as someone who can help them and that's how most people's minds work. They are most likely to talk to you if it benefits them. The downside to this is if they decide to also start a podcast or radio station, they develop the same attitude as seeing you as competition instead of building with you. Not everyone is like that though. I have built relationships with lots of people that do what I do. So let me make it clear that everyone is not like that. You just have to see who's who and with time, they will show who they really are. I have had people who no longer talk to me due to the fact that I decided to do other stuff that was similar to what they are doing. People will try to keep you in a box. People will try to put limitations on you as if you are not supposed to do something that they are doing. A lot of this comes from the mindset of the hood.

WHAT YOU NEED

Now, let's get into some of the things that I've learned along the way that could be helpful and beneficial to you if you are an independent artist. The first mistake that I made when I first started getting into the industry was looking for videographers that were cheap because I wanted to save money. I did not look for previous works that they have done. I didn't look for professionalism and I didn't know all the questions that should be asked before hiring someone to do my video. I found someone on Facebook and we talked over the phone. I saw a couple of videos that actually were not all that good but the urge to get something done as soon as possible overpowered getting it done right. This is mistake number one, NEVER

RUSH. You should take your time when it's your art.

Once I paid my money to this person through PayPal, I quickly saw how unprofessional and ghetto he was. This individual was supposed to sit with me and help me create a treatment for the video. I was putting out a lot of money to book a location, a choreographer and for dancers. I also fed the staff. The videographer began talking to me like I was just some hood person on the street that was not a customer. He became very rude and did not want to meet with me previously before we recorded. He did not want to get together and get the treatment done. And then when I finally said enough is enough, I told him to refund my deposit and I no longer wanted to move forward with him. He then refused to give me my money back and continued to talk to me in a very rude way; he was very disrespectful and unprofessional. This person had no idea that when I do business I do it in a way to protect myself. So I got my money back through my credit card company.

Once they reversed the payment the videographer decided to call and change the tone and attitude but it was too late. I won't waste so much time talking about this unprofessional person but the moral to the story is; do your research before hiring a videographer. Look at their previous works and make sure you're 100% happy with what they did. Do not settle just because you're rushing. Get references, compare pricing to other videographers, and meet up in person before signing or moving forward to see if you can even work with this person taking their character and attitude into consideration. Make sure this person is professional. You should have a long list of questions before hiring them. Here are some basic questions you can ask. Then add whatever else you care about and want and need for your video.

Questions to ask videographers

1. Price

2. Hours of recording time for the price

3. What's included

4. How many people will be shooting

5. What type of camera will be used

6. Will it be done with, HD 1080p red camera Scarlett

7. How many locations can we go to

8. Do you help with promotion

9. Does your price include editing

10. How is payment arrangement set up to get started

11. Are there any contracts and packages that will help me save money

12. Where can I see your work and do you have references

13. Can we meet first before moving forward

14. Do you help create treatment for a video

15. Are props included

16. Do you help get people for the video

17. Do you have any locations we can use

You can add anything from there. Think about what's important to you and write it down that way you know what to ask.

Long story short, I ended up firing him and hiring someone else last minute. The person that I hired worked with big-name people in the industry and one of them was Michael Jackson. This guy was amazing, his energy was great, and he was very professional. He had a full team of people and he made sure that I was comfortable every step of the way. He was extremely expensive though. I guess this is one of those moments where you get what you pay for. He came with a team of people, a lighting crew and a director the whole 9 yards. It was me that was not ready for his professionalism. I say that and laugh before all I hear is Kevin Hart saying nooo she wasn't ready. I just know that I did not want the unprofessionalism from the other guy. However, the video was great and I was actually doing a song that was totally out of my lane and comfort zone which was good because it allowed me to tap in and get outside of the box I was put in. Here are some of the mistakes I made.

Not having a makeup artist or hairdresser on the video shoot. If you are a female or male, you will sweat from working, moving and the bright ass lights that are on you. Your hair could get messed up or fuxxy so you need a hairstylist on deck, or someone who can hold you down while you put in work. You have to keep going because you are on the clock and time is money. You don't have time to keep looking in the mirror or running to the bathroom to fix yourself. You got to stay in action and let the people you hire come fix you up. I did not have that so I was unhappy with the fact that my hair was messed up and my makeup was not perfect. I was also out of shape, so from the previous dancing with heels, my legs were hurting. I was unable to move the way I wanted to. There was a point where I went down and had a hard time getting up.

The shit was funny as hell. Although, not at all times was I embarrassed but when I think about it now, I am cracking the hell up. I was in so much pain that every movement hurts so bad. I honestly didn't even want to do it that day but I had no choice. The place was already paid for and the people were already hired and it was a short time. So my point here is for you to know that you need to be well rested, in shape, have a makeup artist and a hairdresser on site. You also need to have more than one outfit with you. Think about the image you want to put out there. I quickly learned that wigs will always be the go-to for me. Wigs will also be good for you especially if you want different looks in the video.

If you shoot all in one day, that can take over eight hours. So getting several different locks in a video requires a lot of work with being well put together. If you're someone who likes multiple looks, you should go with changing wigs. They are easier and give you a quick fast different look in seconds. You could have wigs already made ready to go, set up and styled so all you have to do is put them on your head and get going. I was not into wigs at the time. I was wearing weaves so I went to get my hair done and by the time it was time to shoot the video, my curls drop in my hair was puffy. My make up was running and I had to keep going because I only had the location for four hours. We were in the heart of Manhattan, a club called Slate. It was the weekend and going overtime at this place was a no-no. It was one of the top clubs in Manhattan. I was able to get in here for a low price because my friend's husband works there. So I paid to use it at a discounted rate. Dealing with a videographer with his level of professionalism taught me a lot. I learned how to deal with and talk to people. I learned that your attitude is what wins you over.

I learn how important it is when you talk to people and the way you talk to people. The way that he made me feel is the way I wanted people to feel when they work with me. So, although he was expensive, I got the job done but I've learned a lot in the process. Learning what I needed from him taught me what to look for in the future from other videographers. And it would then be up to me to decide if I want to work with them. I also have to understand that not everyone will be able to give me everything that he was able to give me because their experiences are different. Some people may be great and just starting out but can still give you a good video. Some people may have some experience but may not be able to produce all that the other videographer was able to do but it doesn't make them substandard. It just means that they may have more experience under your belt to get to that level. We all go through that even as artists when you start out, it takes time to get to a certain point. It doesn't mean that you are no good, just means that you need more experience which will help you grow.

So one of the things that I did not do was get a cover for the song. Album art is very important too. That is what will grab the attention of people before they even listen. Cover art is important because that's what you're going to need when you put the song out. That's what you're going to use when you post on social media. Another thing to know is that you should never give out copies of your main video to anyone. Other people should not be posting your video especially if you are a new artist starting out. If people post a video before you do, no one will take a second look at your video again. It will have to be the hardest thing for people to do. When you're new, your numbers as a matter of necessity need to rise. You are the artist, and you are paying people. They should never put your video out before or after you unless you give the OK. And you really should not give the OK. You should always give out your link. Unless this person is exposing you to a very large crowd of people that will eventually get them to come to you and support and follow you when you're on social media. And they should never share it directly from their social media. It dilutes stuff for the artist. It negatively affects The artist. Everything should lead back to you.

Today we live in a time where the industry is oversaturated with artists. Everybody and their mama want to be an artist. And the Internet has made it easy for everyone to post content on it all day every day. You breaking through all of that is extremely difficult. I'm not saying that it can't be done, I'm just saying that it's difficult. Being able to do that means that you have to have something so incredibly different that it will make people stop and look at yours over everyone else's. That's why you see people doing crazy things on social media for attention or a girl half-naked and twerking just so someone can notice them. Attention seeking is honestly done by all but it's about how you choose to do it. I am not throwing shade but to me, when females expose themselves to get noticed, it stripes them from their dignity. You should also have some promo footage before you post a video. This is how you do a build-up before the video comes out. You should also get some behind-the-scenes shots as well because that is also good for the build-up and promotion.

It gives people a chance to see what's going on behind the scenes and what is to come. It helps people to connect and for it to be in their minds before it comes out. So you expose them to your footage which is now a part of their memory. Your promotion is important, so when the video finally comes out, they would want to see the whole video because they've been hearing and seeing so much about it. I can't lie, I know this information and sometimes still don't do it but I know what my goals are and it really isn't to be an artist. However, I do want to be in the entertainment field. But if you are trying to be an artist, you should do it right. It's totally up to you, you have to be happy with your work so remember when getting the video done, and you should have the attitude that you want the best for yourself. Also, it's better if you pick out your own scene from the video shoot and then allow the videographer to edit it from there. If they pick the scenes they like, it might be different from what you want and this might also show you in a different light that you may not want to be seen. Every shot will not be perfect; that's why taking multiple shots is needed so that you pick the best ones. Some videographers don't like to do that but that is the best way for an independent artist to really get something done the way they want it.

The rule of thumb that I have learned is; don't take too many video shots because when the time comes to pick the scenes, you will feel overwhelmed with trying to select the ones you like. Videographers' always like to get a lot of footage so that they have more footage to work with but if you do too much, it becomes overwhelming for you and for them. Remember that because I learned that the hard way. Nowadays, people like a lot of B roll in their videos so what that does is make it less work for you as the artist to perform these performance shots. You should always make sure you have performance shots, B roll, and shots with you just walking or doing something in reference to your song. The sound does not matter because you do not use the sound of the day of the shoot. You actually use the MP3 and add that to the footage. So it could be noisy and it wouldn't matter.

However, you should have the music that you're going to be using with you and a stereo or speaker so that you can play it out loud for the videographer to know how to line up what you're doing in the words with the music. If you do not have that, it will be extremely hard for them to edit the video. If you're an independent artist and you roll with a very small group of people even by yourself but you are including other people to be a part of your video, then you better do your homework before depending on them. Yes, a lot of people want to be seen and want to be a part of something but it's not their video and it's not their dream. Some people will tell you they're coming and never show up. Always over invite. People come late and people are unprofessional because honestly, they don't need to be because this is not their stuff, music, or brand. If you really want your people to be on time and professional, then you should hire people or use people who are going to school for something specifically based on what you're doing because you know that they will take it seriously. If you can't pay people, offer to feed them and foot transportation bills. Some college students need to do assignments to receive credit for their class. So that's a great way to find people and there will be no out of pocket expense for you. Go online and see what kind of casting businesses are out there to help you find people. Make sure there is someone there that is keeping everything and everyone in order. Otherwise, things could get out-of-control real quick.

A lot of time can be wasted because people and things are not in order and people are not doing what they are supposed to do. This can actually run out your time with the videographer and cost you lots of money. It can also be the reason why you don't get to finish a project. What will happen is you will be rushing through other scenes that were planned because of time wasted due to other people. You must always know who and what you're dealing with when doing business especially when you hire other people to get the job done. If you have someone with a camera or even a cell phone and feel like you want to give it a shot to shoot the video yourself, go for it. A lot of people are doing that now to save money. If you have up to date phones like the iPhone 12 pro max, the cameras on those phones are great and a lot of people use them to shoot videos now. If you know how to do the lighting and angles of the camera and move when you're supposed to move and don't just stand still, then after shooting the video, all you have to do is either edit it yourself or find someone to edit it for you. If you have programs that you Can add effects to your video, that's another great way to complete your video.

This will save you a lot of money all the time but it may also not come out looking as professional as someone who's been doing it for years. You have to know what you're looking for and what you're comfortable with. Some people are not trying to go all out they're just trying to get content out there but sometimes the first impression is everything. You have to want people to want to listen to you or take a second look at you. And if you don't do things right it's a possibility that they may not even take you seriously or look at you again. So whatever you do just make sure that it looks good and make sure you are happy with it. Make sure you get other opinions as well because everyone has a different point of you and you don't want to base everything off of one person, so get several opinions if you can. Try not to say what you think first, let them use their own brain. A lot of times, we tell people what it is that we like or don't like and that affects their judgement. Let them think on their own.

Remember I told you people tend to follow what other people say. If you're sitting somewhere and listening to something and no one Bobs their head and then all of a sudden someone starts bobbing his/her head, other people see it most likely they will start bobbing their head. I'm not saying everyone would do this but most people will because most people follow. How many times have you turned on the radio, hated a song or heard someone say they hate a song and then later within a week or two they're singing and dancing to it. Well maybe you're singing it and dancing to it. It's all a part of programming. Now that's just a few things about getting a video done let's talk about dealing with these producers. Oh Boy here we go. You might need to get some wine or sip some tea because the game has changed thoroughly. It is not what it used to be.

The artist is being jerked left and right, up and down all around. It has turned into a joke in the artist industry. This is another reason why I don't even want to participate in being an artist. I rather be on the other side of the table owning everything and keeping my rights to everything that I do. Artists are the ones who work hard and put in the sweat equity while everyone else around them gets paid from the artist's talent. It's a harsh reality of this music game. But I understand nobody will come around and work for free. You're lucky if you got a team of people that believe in you and are willing to do that. However in this industry, when it comes to getting beat, if you're an independent artist that does not have a personal relationship with a producer that is willing to work with you directly for the come up for both of you, you're going to find yourself in a lot of bullshit. Let me explain to you what I mean about this.

MORE OF WHAT YOU NEED TO KNOW

First, let me tell you there are some producers out there that still have done a lot in this industry where they're not giving away their beats for cheap. I can understand that. When you created a name for yourself, had platinum records and been in the game for years, and you know your worth. No one can tell you what you're worth and I get that but people should not be doing what they are doing to these artists nowadays because they see that this is an oversaturated industry of millions and trillions of people trying to become artists and use that to their advantage. These producers will sell you a beat and sell it to millions of other people. You do all the work as the artist, put it out and everyone will receive royalties from it. They charge you for a beat and then they lease it to you and then turn around and do the same thing to anybody else who wants the same beat. They are getting paid for the same thing over and over again. It's a hustle and disgrace at the same time. It can only happen because artists allow it, they are desperate for beats. Not only that the contracts are ridiculous to me, it's worse than getting jerked by record labels.

And you must be careful, they will put a beat online and sell it to millions of people and still have it for sale as an exclusive beat. So what does that mean? It simply means that if you buy a beat at any time and someone could have possibly bought it before you, they have leasing rights to use it. You would have to legally approach the situation which can cost you even more money because you're going to need a lawyer. You have to request these people who have the beat to remove it and take it down. Now you will run into issues because they paid for the leasing rights. These producers could care less. They probably figure out what the hell most of these people are never going to make it anyway or they probably are not even going to have the money to get legal representation to request for the other artist to take it down. So what does that mean? It simply means that you and a whole bunch of other artists can have the same beat, record to the same beat with equal leasing right thereby undermining the authenticity of each individual artist.

The producers have become the new people when it comes to jerking the artist nowadays. Imagine making a dope song, being so happy and proud of it, investing money, supporting this song, promoting it and then you hear other people using the same beat. It is a disaster and it's heartbreaking for an artist. It takes away your individuality of the sound. And it's even worse if you purchase a beat with the hook. Oh my God! now not only do you have another artist on it, you have other artists using it with the same hook and now you just sound like a feature. You still have to pay the producer their royalties as well as the artist that's on the beat. Most of the time, these producers get writers' credit if they sell you a beat with the hook because they're giving you A beat with words on it.

Read your contracts people. This is a dirty grimy industry. No one respects the artist. Everyone just wants to use the artist, get free entertainment and take every dime they get. It is a damn shame. Everyone around them just wants to know how they are going to get paid. All of this is based on the artist's talent and what they do. Everyone uses that individual. It is sad. Then you have to be careful when it comes to publishing because a lot of producers own publishing part of that too. They will tell you that they made the music and they deserve half of the publishing. This is not true. Remember I told you a contract is what you negotiate. You can buy a beat outright and own that beat and that beat can be yours or you can just give credit on the album. You don't have to give up publishing. We will talk about publishing a little later. I just want to quickly address some of that. If you're an artist, the best advice I can give you is; learn how to make your own beats. Otherwise, get ready to get jerked if you don't know a producer willing to work with you one on one and make beats exclusively for you where you work together as a team. If you're buying beats or getting them offline, get ready cause shit is going to hit the fan and you are going to get played.

I know a lot of producers are going to be pissed about this and probably hate me for saying it and guess what I don't give a damn. Do you know why I don't give a damn because I've been a victim to this and I know how it feels. So my job is to help other artists not make the same mistakes that I've made. These producers have made other artists feel like they don't even want to be artists anymore, that's how bad it is. I felt like that a couple of times because of them. It's a shame that someone's greed can destroy someone's dream. Now, let's talk about putting out a single or album. I want to give some advice on some of the things you need to do and know before putting out a single or an album. The first thing is; who is your target audience. This is important so you know to whom you are marketing and promoting. You can't promote to the wrong people because then it would make it seem like you are unwanted. Remember people have different opinions. So you have to know who you will be marketing to.

I can't tell you how to record your song. You have to do that. Meaning you have to know if you'd like to write it and record or just go in and freestyle or just go in and see what comes out of it. Whatever you do, just remember that you might be asked to perform this song. And if that happens, then you have to be ready. Now let's talk about putting out a single. Here are all the things that we are going to need first: your lyrics, are you the writer? Then you're going to need a beat which is a track either the MP3 or the tracked out stems. The difference between the two is that the MP3 is a compressed file where everything is together and cannot be separated. Therefore, if you mix it, that would be mixed as one track in your voice and vocals will be mixed as a separate track. When you have the stems and someone mixes them, they can mix each individual instrument separately. This allows them to have more access to mixing it better.

It gives the engineer more control to do what they want and move around the way they want with the track. Now the next thing you're going to need is a place to record your music after you've written to the track. You're going to obviously need a studio to record or you can do it at home if you have what you need to do so. Most people use ProTools but there are a lot of other programs out there that other people use and say are better. After you have recorded the song, you're going to need to get this song mixed and mastered. Once this song is mixed and mastered, then you're going to have to find out how you will put it out. This means that you will have to find a distributing company to get all of your music on all of the platforms. I'm going to get into that later. Once you choose a company that you want to use to get on the streaming platforms then you must gather everything you need to put it out.

You're obviously going to need an art cover for this single or album. You're going to need some type of money to promote it. Doing interviews with people to get it out there. That's just the basics. The most important part of all of this is your promotion money. If you just do that and you are a new artist, no one would know who you are or that you even exist and they won't be looking for you because they don't know you. So you have to get people to know you. How do you do that? You have to promote yourself heavily. If you don't then you would just have a great song sitting on all these platforms not doing anything for you. If you don't have the hookup or the plug then you better have a lot of promotion money.

And even if you do have the hookup and the plug, you still better have promotion and marketing money. Let's talk about doing shows now. When you have music and you're doing shows, you should have flyers and business cards. It's also nice to have T-shirts and to also give stuff like that away to people who purchase your album or to those who may stream or are fans of yours. Here's the ugly side of performing as an independent artist. Everyone expects you to do this job for free. No one respects you and no one wants to pay you but they want to be entertained by you. It's almost like you have to prove yourself to them. Actually, it's not almost, you do. The sad part is a lot of these people that do the shows in these promoters will charge at the door to get money then promote the show with you being an entertainer and not pay you a damn dime. It is pathetic and sad.

Then if you speak up about it and tell them that you should get something for your time and your entertainment, they will tell you that no one knows who you are and you are not bringing people into the club therefore you should not get anything. This type of thing has been happening and is still happening now the only way it will change is if you as the artist change it. If you don't know your worth, nobody else does either. So, the promoters won't pay you upfront money with no one knowing you and you are possibly not bringing in a crowd. That doesn't seem fair to the promoter. Most promoters have to pay for the building and try to recoup their money back with a profit. This is understandable. But it is just plain ole greedy to have people coming in watching someone entertain and perform and give them absolutely nothing. If you let them be a part of what you got going on and you asked them to be a part of what is going on then, that means you see value in them.

All of a sudden you want to tell them they hold no value when it's time to get paid. That's another way to fuck people over. Make you feel like you're not worth it. Well, what I say to that is; you independent artists out there, get the place yourself, perform and sell tickets. You don't need someone to do that for you, you can do it on your own if you are serious about your business. If someone wanted to be a fair promoter, get their profit and use you as entertainment for the people then they should let you sell tickets and let you take half. The best way to go about it is to get the artist tickets to sell. Let them keep half of the money from the tickets. That will be their upfront money for the show. Anyone that comes in after that that says they're there to see that person perform. The artist should get half of that money. That part is hard because now you have to trust that the promoter will give you that portion of the money but there's a way that you can actually be fair to the artist and give them a little something for their time even if it's $50, I don't care. They should always get something.

Correction, we should get something. Anytime you are doing anything and your time is involved, you have to find out what value it holds. If it's not monetary, then what can I give you of value that would replace your time and sweat equity? This is up to you to determine. But it is understood that some people just want to get seen and heard and are willing to do anything and don't care about getting paid. I can understand that part too if you make that choice but if you find yourself getting frustrated feeling overworked and unappreciated then that means you need to make changes. That means that you feel you are devalued and that it's up to you to fix it. No one will ever fix that for you. They will use you and handle you the way you let them. Trust me,

I know it happens to me all time. Always remember that people can only do to you what you allow them to do to you. If you constantly show that you have no value and you Are worth nothing, they will treat you like that forever. The minute you speak up, they will make you look like you're the bad person. And will point out flaws to devalue you so they can continue to use you.

And as I stated before, the minute you say what you're worth, they will quickly try to remind you how you're not worth anything and people don't know you. Don't fall for the banana in the tailpipe bullshit. My thing is if I'm worth nothing and no one cares that I'm there then guess what you don't need me then. And as I earlier stated, no one and I mean no one is your friend for real. My biggest mistake was thinking that people were my friends and none of them was, absolutely none. They all had their own agenda. Some people will come across as if they are trying to help you but the truth is they're really just using you for their own benefit. They may give a little but take a lot. They will give you just enough to make you feel like you are appreciated. When really when they're giving you something it ain't worth what you're giving them. I had so many people tell me about other people using me when they were doing the same thing. My friend told me to study the snake. So I've been doing that and you should too. So the moral to that story is; it's better to just get a couple of the other independent artists together, put in some money, rent out a venue, sell y'all tickets, make your money, promote yourselves, that's what you're there for anyway.

Now let's talk about doing features on other peoples songs. This can get tricky. It can get tricky because paperwork should always be done first. I have made this mistake several times before. If you do not get the paperwork done before you actually send off work that you've done to be featured on someone else's stuff, you risk the chance of not getting paid for your work. You never know can blow up big and make millions and if you don't have your stuff in order to prove that you are supposed to get compensated for your work you could end up not getting anything. It will be a lot of work to try to hire a lawyer and fight for what you think you deserve and it will be hard to say what you deserve if you don't have paperwork upfront. This should always be negotiated at the time of being asked if you would do the feature. You should know what percentage you want as a writer, what credit you want on the album and if you want any publishing.

Most people will get upset when you ask for that stuff considering they don't even handle their stuff professionally and don't know anything about doing paperwork. Some people's intentions are to get over on you and take full credit for everything, even your rhymes and your performance on the song. If you are a writer and you're also performing a song on the track, they are two separate jobs. You need to know that. If you are an artist and have someone else write the song with you, the writer is going to want their credit unless they sold you the song. Now that should help you understand that even if you are an artist that wrote the song they are two separate jobs. What that means is you should get two separate checks, not separate checks coming from the person that you did the contract with but coming from distribution and the performance rights organization. There are three major performance rights organizations BMI, ASCAP, and Seasac.

Those companies are the places where you register every song that you do. This is so when your song gets on streaming platforms that you receive a check. This also makes you look more professional as an artist. If you're just someone recording in your basement or your home and not doing anything with the music, just to look famous, then you're not taking the job seriously. If you are a writer or an artist that is recording, you should definitely sign up to a performance by the organization. This is another great way to show people you mean business. Also, it's another great way to explain why you need a contract before you do or send off any work. The great thing about being a part of these organizations is that if you are performing a song and that place is registered with a performance rights organization, you can input that information into the system that you performed that song there and they will make sure you get paid. There are so many ways for you to get paid as an artist, you just have to do your research and find out how. Now let's talk about publishing real quick. I have my own publishing company and use it strictly for myself although I can offer these services to other artists. Publishing is important.. Most record labels own the publishing of their artists. That's not good. The artist should have at least some of their own publishing.

When the artist finds out and then realizes how much money was made and what they walked away with versus the labels walking away with all the publishing, the artist becomes upset and wants to fight to get the publishing. You can look up a lot of artists that have been broke and jerked by people who took all the publishing. It is important to own your own masters to everything that you have unless you're willing to sacrifice and give it up for something else. Owning your publishing company is the same as owning an LLC. It's a business. But it's a business where you get paid more money in addition to what you would get paid from the performance rights organization and a distributing company.

When you're negotiating with people, you don't want to leave out publishing. If you want more money and more control over what you do, then what you want is your all publishing company. If you are the type of person who doesn't want to have to worry about doing the paperwork, following up and handling business and just want to do music and go about your business, then none of these things matter. But just know that anyone else that's willing to do this for you is looking to receive a hefty bonus.

Don't get me wrong, you may get lucky with getting someone who wants to help you. I have done things for many people and expect nothing in return. However, I ran into a lot of people who do not want to help me because that is the way that they personally are. The crabs in a barrel mentality. People like to see you doing good but you just can't do better than them. Then you become a threat and a competitor. I noticed that I built more relationships when I was no longer considered someone in the same line of business as them. Even outside of the music industry and other types of businesses, people are nice and friendly until you start doing what they are doing. Mainly our people, when I say our people I mean black people. I'm just going to put that out there. We're not sugarcoating anything, we're keeping it real and direct. This is exactly why in this genre which is hip-hop music you will find many issues.

It's not to say that other genres of music don't have issues, it's just that you will get that mentality of what we all know to be crabs in a barrel. But in this game, there are vultures everywhere. And it's not just in hip-hop, but in today's time, hip-hop is extremely oversaturated. Everybody wants to rap no matter what color you are. The great thing about hip-hop is that culture influences everything and everybody all over the world. That's why everyone wants to be a part of it. But people want to use and abuse those that are participating in it. Even some may want to be a part of it and rap the culture and benefit from it but give nothing back to the people that supported them.

When you are a female in this industry, it can even be harder. Hard because you have a lot of people that think that you don't know anything and will try to take a vantage of you. Most people think that you would use what you got to get what you want. Don't get me wrong, some people will use what they got to get what they want. But not everyone will do that. But everyone will get treated like they do that. This is sad because most females in this industry get taken advantage of and played. They are used as sexual beings for sexual desires and that's it. In order to get on, they will be expected to do sexual favors in return and this is extremely important why you should know the business when it comes to your music. Being an artist is a huge responsibility. You must and I say it again you must know the business. It is not just about being an artist, it's about building a brand. Honestly, most artists don't really make a lot of money. A lot of them get their money from other deals that are offered to them. They get sponsorships and other opportunities.

The sponsorships that they get are what helps them make money but they get them because they have already created a brand. When you create a brand, people start looking at you. This is why you have to be careful what you say and what you do unless you really just don't give a damn. And sometimes, that even works for a lot of artists out there who put themselves out there to talk about how they want and a lot of companies are still investing in them. Why because they have a large following. It's all about your following. Everyone will follow with everyone else. This is how the industry works. Let's talk about following for a minute.

Numbers have become the new talent. This is why you will see a lot of people on the Internet doing ridiculous kinds of stuff just to be seen. They need to do things that are outrageous to get people to tune in. Being regular and doing regular stuff just won't work. This is where you will find your girls twerking, guys playing with guns, people there doing crazy things and saying random stuff for attention. People would do anything for numbers. Talent alone is not going to cut it sadly. You have to be doing something that no one else is doing. But the sad part to that everyone is doing exactly what I just mentioned, playing with guns, being ridiculous and saying dumb things to get noticed, recording fights in the street, and people are actually tuning in and watching that stuff.

So then, I guess the question becomes; is it really about doing something crazy, or is it just what people want to see? When you think about it, we're living in a time that is oversaturated with several artists. They claim that everyone sounds the same. However, everyone that's doing the same crazy outlandish things on the Internet still seems to get the views. So which one is it? I guess that's for you to figure out because I haven't figured out that part yet. The only thing I can say is; I know that people that do those crazy things get more views. But a lot of people are waking up and trying to focus on the talent. Going back to artist development is extremely important. Most companies in record labels do not want to Develop an artist. They want the artist to already be fully developed before they put them on. Now the question is; once the artist already built the fan base, why would they need a record label? Well, that boils down to money. As I stated before, a record label puts out money for the artist, they help them get shows, they have a bigger reach and they can do bigger things that an artist may not be able to do or have the money to do. You must remember; this is a business and it is an investment. So someone may see you to be a profitable person and that's why they want to invest in you. This is how it works and always has. No one is your friend or trying to help you. They're trying to get paid too. Remember that and don't you ever forget it.

Now let's get back to the numbers. And let's talk about why people look for numbers. As I stated, people look for numbers because they want to see if you have a fan base. However, the sad part about this is that there's always a way to get around that. Buying numbers is what a lot of artists do. It makes them look good but let's be honest, they are only fooling themselves. When you buy numbers, you are buying a bunch of fake fans. No one really likes, listening or paying attention to you. It's a bunch of fake accounts or people who have no interest in you. This is bad for business. However, people still do it because it makes them look good. The part where it works is that other people see that your numbers are high assuming that you're doing big things and popular, have a huge fan base and from that, they will follow you. They are going off of a lie that you created.

So yes, it may benefit you to gain followers who follow what other people do because they think you already have a lot of people that are interested in you. That goes back to what I said earlier, people follow what other people do, they tend not to make their own decisions on their own. But here's how it can hurt you. When you buy followers, if a platform finds out, they can shut your account down. When you are posting and trying to reach potential brands or customers, it may be targeted to all your fake phony followers. This means it does not get to the right people that will truly support you and that are truly your fans. So when you understand how social media works, then you'll get it. Let me give you a little understanding of that. Facebook, Instagram and other sites use algorithms. They will choose 20% or less of your friends or followers to see your actual post.

It is based on the quantity of access you're getting from that post that will allow it to reach more people. If the post is not getting that much attention, they assume it's not popular enough and people don't want to see it so they do not put it in front of other people. If they feel the post is getting a lot of attention, then they will let other people see it. Remember, there's a benefit in it for them as well. So what all that means is that if you post something and you have a bunch of fake followers, they may pick 20% or less of your fake friends and fake followers to see your post. You will not get the attention that you were hoping that post would get, therefore they will restrict it from reaching other people and real supporters. This is why buying followers actually hurts you more than it helps you. Again, all it does is create a fake façade for you to look good to other people. You're only fooling yourself when you do this. It is not good for business. And most people can tell that you bought the followers if they look through your account. How can they do this?

By simply going on these accounts and seeing how they have thousands of people that they are following hardly any other followers. Then you may see a couple of pictures on their page of random pictures that they pulled off the Internet just to have someone looking like they posted something. When you see that many followers, those are all the people who bought into the fake followers. Definitely not a good look. Sometimes you may even pay a company and think it's legit and they will tell you that you will gain real followers and they will give you many followers but it's a lie. Trust me, I know I've been there. These people are telling you they are real organic followers but they are not.

They will tell you they will give you real likes from targeting real people but they are the one using the system and bots to get likes on your photos. Again, It may help to get your post in front of other people but the algorithm will pick that up and think that those accounts want to see your post and they will start targeting them instead of your real fan base. You do not want to do this. I'm advising you to stay away from doing that. If you have 100 people on your page that are following you and they're organic, that is better than having 10,000 fake followers. Just think about it, 1000 people standing in line that don't want your product and 100 people that do. Where will you sell your product? To the hundred people I hope. And think about the profit you can make from selling to 100 people versus not selling to 10,000. It doesn't matter how big the crowd is, it matters about who is spending money and supporting you. That's how you know how well you're doing with your brand with your business and with your music.

So now let's get into how you should be moving as an artist. let's talk about the important parts of developing yourself as a professional. As I stated before, having your business in order, having the paperwork right, registering with a performance rights organization, getting your logo, having a website creating your social media, all of these are important. All of those show that you are investing in yourself and in your brand. It is now time to talk about your attitude. Attitude is key, most people think they need to show this brave bald aggressive person but that is actually a turn-off. You do want to show people that you're not to be played with. However, you don't want to push people away. Having an ego in this game can actually be more harmful to you than you think. It's OK to be confident and know that you're good but you should also be humble. Building relationships is extremely important. This is important because everyone does have the attitude no matter what you think they feel like; what am I getting out of this relationship. Everyone wants something. I'm going to keep saying that because I want you to remember that.

I don't care if somebody gets mad, it is the truth and I'm sticking to that. Now showing up on time to your appointments is important. Being able to speak professionally is important. Not soliciting your music is important. It is also important to build relationships by helping others is important and not just thinking of yourself. All of these things are helpful in putting yourself out there. People like to see that you're not selfish and that it's just not all about yourself. They also like humble people. If you come in like I don't need you, I'm the shit I'm better than you, you will turn people off. I know so many artists that were great and their attitudes got in the way and it didn't help them move forward at all. Most people will not want to deal with someone who has an attitude like that. While they are standing still and doing certain things to get noticed, that is degrading. I didn't have to do any of that when I sold my personality. That's it, I was able to do that and still keep my dignity and show that I have morals. That was my key selling point to building my career, just be myself. People will always remember how you treated them and how you made them feel. If you leave a bad impression, they will never forget that. So even if you have a nasty attitude, you better work on fixing it especially in this industry. Or else you will get more enemies than fans. And you will get more enemies than supporters.

So overall, the moral to the short book is this, as independent artists, we struggle with a lot of things but a lot of times, the struggle can come from your own doings. We have to know how to represent ourselves in a professional manner. You have to work on building your brand and not just thinking about being an artist. Part of that comes with investing in yourself and making sure you have a humble attitude. You need to know the business when doing this and if you do not, people will take advantage of you. You have to be willing and ready to do what you need to do to get seen and heard and what I mean by that is; you have to be ready to invest your time, blood sweat and tears, Late nights and preparedness for disappointments. Be ready for everyone to tell you what you should be doing and how you should be doing it. Some people condemned me and spoke ill of what I am doing and what I preach.

I was even disrespected by my family and insulted because I spoke of black unity when people wanted gangster talk. When they saw it was working for me, they started to change their attitude and language. People who know you will not believe in you until they see others do. It's so much that you have to think and worry about but if you want to make it, that's part of the game. The most important thing that you really need to know is what you want out of this whole game. That right there would determine how you move forward. Some people just get into this because they love it and they have no idea what they want from it. Then you can find yourself competing with someone who has a different goal than you do. Never get caught up in that situation that will set you back. Not only will it set you back, it will have you working toward something that you don't even want. You can work hard and get it and be miserable because it's not what you wanted in the first place.

So, know what it is that you want. Know what it is that makes you happy. Know who your real friends are and know who a true team is. Be around people who believe in you and what you do. Pay attention to how they act and how they talk about you. Do they brag about your music, do they play it or do they just come around just to chill? Do they play everybody else stuff and not play yours. If they are not playing your music like they played other people's music on the radio, they don't truly believe in you. They may not really like your music or like your stuff; they're just hoping that it takes off because it will benefit them as well. You can always tell who truly believes in you by the way they respond to your music.

Some people will help you and don't even like your stuff. So what do you want out of this? Let's see. Maybe you want to be rich and famous? How are you going to do that? Maybe you realize that you love writing music but you don't like to be an artist. This can happen. It happened to me. I used to love to be an artist but then I realized that I don't like doing shows and I dislike going to perform and exhaust energy when I only wanted to enjoy the show. I know that I like to create music and I love it. But I know that I don't want to be traveling all around just to work. This is a job and you have to remember that. Traveling all around the world to perform does not mean you're chilling, it means you're working. Some people just look at the TV and think that it's all fun and games and everybody's having a great time but their asses have to sweat and they're not sleeping. They go from one state to the next state and they are performing. Even when you're tired, you expected to put on a good show. In a minute you don't, you will be criticized, talked about and made fun of. This is the industry. You also should know you have to remember that you will no longer have a private life and your business will be out there for the world to see. There's no more walking out the house without your wig or make up or for guys in your holy sweats.

People are watching, people are looking, people are talking, people are filming. Your private life is over. Can you deal with that, do you want to deal with that? Every mistake you make will be on the front line for the world to see and talk about. You will be on the front line and so will your loved ones. They will be talking about your family, your mother, your grandmother, your kids and even your dog. No one cares about your feelings. They simply don't. The minute that you say one thing, you'll lose all your sponsors if they don't agree with it. How are you going to deal with that? Do you have what it takes to sustain this industry?

If you don't, then you have to reconsider your intention to become an artist. Maybe you might just want to be in the background, be a writer, talk your shit, make your mistakes, have your private life but still be rich. Is it about the money because if it's about the money then you might want to find out what it's like to be behind the scenes. If it's about the money you might want to look into sync licensing and see about getting your music on commercials, movies, TV shows and video games. That is the direction I made up my mind to move in. However, I still do feature songs for other people if they ask him to but I have no interest in being an artist. But if someone wants to pay me for a feature then guess what?

You've got yourself an artist. And I know how to conduct myself as a professional artist when it's time to. But that cannot be my number one goal and they cannot be what's in the forefront. It's in the back but I'm still creating and doing what I love. So once again, what I'm trying to tell you is; know what it is that you want in this game. Do not get caught up in what everyone else's reality of success is. That will have you running around like a chicken with your head cut off. Know what you want to do so that you don't get off track and don't let people make you lose focus on what your goal is. Also remember that everyone's going to have an opinion. Everyone is going to tell you what you should be doing and how it should be done. Most of these people never did it before. They think that what worked for someone else will work for you.

Wrong, that is absolutely not true. Some people have to work hard to get into this industry, some people shake their ass just enough for people to get noticed. Some people may do something totally crazy just to get someone's attention so that people will give them a record deal. "Catch me outside", remember her. It doesn't take much. Remember nobody got time for that. Doesn't take much. But it went viral. People liked it, people listened to it and guess what? It made her famous. Then you have those who worked so hard and so professional and it worked for them. Then you have those who try to do one thing or the other and none of it worked. Sometimes it's just about luck. It's also about who you know.

Who you know means a lot. And let me make sure I'm clear on who you know means a lot when they have the power to make moves. But knowing someone who is famous without power to make moves does nothing for you. This is because most people that are artists like you don't have any pull, just street cred. Most people are impressed with that. They don't have any control over anything and someone is actually putting them on so that they can eat. The only thing they have is fame. Most people just want that. And for the ones who do, they get it and someone else to get rich. They get taken advantage of. But that's what they wanted so that's what they got. That's why you must know what you want. It's nobody's fault if you tell someone I just want to be famous for people to know my name well and someone will help you with that. People will know your name and you will be famous. And that's what you will get. People will scream your name and you will be famous and you will get what you wanted. Someone that helps you get all of that is now receiving the financial benefits from it because that's what they wanted; the monetary part. So what you ask for, you get. They got what they wanted. Who's fault is it? No one's but yours because you stated what you wanted and you got what you asked for. You should be happy right?

KNOW YOUR CODES AND NUMBERS

So again at the end of the day, protect yourself. Get a good lawyer. Don't accept the same lawyer as them. If someone wants to do business and they say they know a lawyer do not use that lawyer. Find your own. That lawyer may work in their best interest and it is a conflict of interest. However, be very careful some lawyers are drawing up label-friendly deals so they build relationships with labels to get more clients but the artist is paying for the service. As I earlier stated, it's a dirty game. These are just some of the basic things that you need to know and pay attention to if you don't already know. But you have to remember to keep your eye on the prize, whatever that is for you. Down below, I'm going to give you a list of places where you can actually get yourself on the right track as an artist when it comes to being professional and having your paperwork in order.

And remember record labels are not bad; they're only investing in something that they feel they can make a profit from. If you don't have any money to invest in yourself and your career, then you will need a record label to do that. If you have the money you can do it on your own but it is a lot of hard work. You will need money to get your songs on the radio. Unfortunately, we live in a time where it's all about the money now not about the talent and you have to remember that. Most artists were able to come up off of drug deals. That's not something you should be doing, you don't want to put your life on the line for a career that you might never get a chance to do because you were out there doing something illegal. But you will hear that was the story for many. Although they may have got away with it and it worked for them, that doesn't mean it would work for you. So, please keep that in mind when you are doing what you do whatever that may be.

Remember the hardest part of this music business is not just finding the producers with affordable dope ass beats or coming up with great ideas for your songs, It's not just about building a fan base or getting DJs to play your music and get mentioned in blogs to support you. It's not about numbers and followers you got on social media. Although you should plan out the marketing and promotions for your release and then launch your campaign, it's bigger than that too. Having a team of people who will help you is a plus in this industry. But there is something just as important that you should know about representing yourself as an artist, brand and business. The hard part is grinding and putting in the work. Most people talk the talk but don't walk the walk. They act and pretend for social media. They get people involved and have all these meetups and nothing ever happens. Life has a way to distract you and what will you do to make sure this doesn't happen because at the end of the day, no one remembers how you started but they never forget how you ended up. So don't allow excuses to be your way out.

Some people invest more money in weed, drinks and partying and then expect others to invest in them when they haven't done it themselves. They are already celebrating before they win anything. Yes, you have to do what you need to survive but until you make it, you are going to have to do that anyway so why not focus on your dream in the process and stop complaining and coming up with mad excuses. Yes, some things are unfair, that's a part of life. Yes, there are people out there who you are better off. So what. Don't put your time and energy in the wrong place.

Put your time and energy into creating your music and putting it out online and on streaming platforms. Also, do direct sales. You must always promote and market your brand and gain new active fans. You gotta beat the streets. Get out there and engage with your fans, hand out your music, hang up posters, take photos and be ready to perform everywhere you can. Some people still sell CDs.. Shout out to the pop the trunk era people. Being seen and constantly staying in people's minds so they remember who you are and what you do is all part of the process. Build relationships and network, network, network by showing up at clubs and events where your fans hang out. Things are always changing, new platforms are always popping up, so stay on top of what's popping and what's new. Knowing this is only half the battle of what you have to actually do it.

The PRO that I discussed before such as ASCAP/BMI is only American rights protection. But there are ways to collect outside the US such as Canada, South Africa, U.K, Australia, Germany, and London. This is the part you must research. Learning about Sync royalties is what I am now focused on. Sync royalties are collected when your music is licensed to TV shows, commercials for both TV and film, video games, and Smartphone apps. Print royalties include lyrical reprints, guitar tabs, and even music sheet books. So when your lyrics are used, you earn money. You may have back pay waiting in an unclaimed account and not even know it. The key is to learn the royalty collection system, data recognition and other accounts that you can run yourself independently. When you are doing business, always have a lawyer to look over your contract. Keep in mind you may be chasing after someone else's clout , and it will not help your career at all. You will have street cred and fame and that shit ain't paying any bills. Don't believe the hype.

Know and learn the game because it's going to take more than just being good to make it. You must take time to learn the business and how to play the game. Having a PRO account is not the only thing you need to do when it comes to getting your paperwork in order. The Pro pays the songwriter and Publishing. These companies such as CD Baby which is the one I used and Tunecore are distributors. I use CD Baby because they have the Pro package where they do all your sound exchange, harry fox, etc for you. SoundExchange is a non-interactive list. It pays the person who owns the masters and performance artist. Learn the data and codes and what they mean so that you are able to conduct your business as an artist properly. Then go into each account and begin to register.

Learn how to monetize many different ways off of one song. It can add up quickly if you do it right. Below, I am going to give you some codes you should know and what the codes mean. Please keep in mind, I don't know everything so there may even be other stuff out there that I didn't mention, so do your research. However, knowing this will give you a huge head start in the game. It will definitely fill your pockets and bank account with cash instead of you receiving nothing just waiting on streams alone. First, I would like to mention that you should self publish if you can. Copyright your Lyric and audio because that is also a way to track and monetize off of your song and music.

CODES YOU SHOULD KNOW

1. Songwriter: IPI- Interested Parties Information number A Social security number for you as the songwriter

2. ISRC - International Standard Recording Code- Like a social security number for the actual recording- It is different for radio version remixes etc. It Tracks sales for your single.

3. MOC - Music On Console - A way to listen to music on a terminal base music player.

4. Performing Artist: If you are performing the song but didn't write it

5. Gracenotes- is a database that provides data for tons of different music services. If you ever use the voice command in the car asking it to play a song that is how it is tracked

6. Media BDS is for Song register

7. UPC - Universal Product Code- is the package for IRSC codes of your Album or Ep like a cd. Tracks all sales from that one unit sold.

8. UPC is done in SOUNDSCAN:

9. Composer - Someone who writes the music

10. Distribution: CD BABY

11. Aggregator PRO - the easy way for people to find the hottest trending video and content in your genre and share it to your social sites.

12. Publisher: CAE - Composers, Authors and Publishers same as IPI CAE is getting phased out.

13. ISWC- International standard work code -is like a social security number for you song - it tracks royalties that is owe to each individual songwriter to that song

14. PRO. Performance Rights Organization will issue your ISWC code and IPI number

You should create a document file or zip file with all your code for each song so that when and if you need to fill out the paperwork for SoundExchange you have them.

Let us go over how the streaming pays. Here is an example of that.

Artists Normally earn about $0.00217 per stream. Your song needs to be streamed 456 times to make $0.99, the typical price of an iTunes download. That's just flat out ridiculous to me. According to the infographic, Spotify, which is a typical reference point for most artists, pays artists about $0.003 per stream which equates to 330 streams being equal to one $0.99 download. However, on Spotify's website, they claim the spread is $0.006 to $0.0084 for an average of $0.0072 or 137 streams per $0.99. Spotify also does not pay on a per-stream basis. So what are we so stuck on pushing Spotify? Their formula takes into account their monthly subscription revenues and an artist's overall popularity which I think is a bunch of bullshit but to each his own.

Now let's analyze what that actually means. There are two key differences between streams and purchases: downloads we need to go over. When you purchase a download, you pay upfront for the ability to listen to the song an unlimited number of times. When you are listening to a stream on Spotify or other streaming services, the royalty is allocated on a pay as you go plan. If someone was to purchase the song for $0.99, do you actually think they would listen to it at least 456 times? I don't. Also, keep in mind that artists do not receive the full $0.99 from a download and this is why I stress doing direct sales.

Let's compare the numbers in the form of RPMs, which is revenue per 1,000 impressions, a common metric used across the digital advertising industry. According to the infographic, RPMs earn artists an average of $2.17 and are as high as $8.10 to $10 on Deezer and Radio, respectively. On Spotify, RPMs are, on average, as high as $7.20 according to their website. So when we compare, music doesn't have the lowest RPMs for digital impressions and is right in line with industry standards. Let's look at what some of the artists we know made from streaming.

- The Monster Eminem -35.1 million streams, $210,000 – $294,000

- Timber Pitbull -32.0 million streams, $192,000 – $269,000

- Royals Lorde -65.3 million streams, $392,000 – $549,000

- Counting Stars One Republic -57.7 million streams, $346,000 – $484,000

- Hey Brother Avicii -46.5 million streams, $279,000 – $391,000

- Wrecking Ball Miley Cyrus -60.4 million streams, $363,000 – $508,000

- Roar Katy Perry -64.6 million streams, $388,000 – $543,000

- Wake Me Up Avicii -152.1 million streams, $913,000 – $1.3 million

- Hold On, We're Going Home Drake -47.1 million streams, $283,000 – $396,000

- Burn Ellie Goulding -53.8 million streams, $323,000 – $452,000

Let's not forget about live music. There has been tremendous growth in live music and concerts, with many indicating that this is where artists will earn the bulk of their revenue. So most artists get money from shows. So these sneaky Record Companies have added clauses in the artist contract and made it a part of their 360 deals. Back in the day, the goal of touring was to promote album sales, but with an explosion of music festivals in recent years, live concerts have become a huge focal point for artists to earn revenue. Revenues from live concerts are split between the concert promoters such as Live Nation, Artists, and Labels.

Some indies pay to perform and open up for big-name artists for exposure. Big-name artists get paid big bucks to perform. The way to make money is for you to try to actually turn every live show into a potential music sale by recording every show and selling the downloads. Up and coming artists, especially, are not making money to perform live; they are spending money instead.

You are always either spending money or splitting the money with someone. Even if you publish yourself, iTunes takes 1.2% Google play takes 2% so you start at 80-90%. Universal could have a deal with Sony and Sony could be asking for 50%. Now you're at 7.5% of your sales revenue from your label. And they damn sure are going to take their cut before you get yours. That's why a signed artist makes on average 16% of their sales revenue whereas you could make more if you released it and own yourself because after the sites and stream services take their percentage which is rightfully so a non-signed artist makes roughly 86% which is the full profit of all your sales distributions. 100% in music report licensing deals. 100% copyright owner and performer. See why ownership is important? If you were signed you would probably get 5-10% performing artists and no copyright percentage.

YouTube counts a "view" anytime someone watches your video for 30 seconds or more. On Facebook, they count a "view" as 3 seconds or more. To earn a YouTube view a user has to watch 10 times more of your video than on Facebook. Facebook is 15 Seconds to get Adsense. But they now have so many rules and restrictions it may affect the artist from getting money. Here is how the payout works depending on where it's coming from.

- Background Singers - SE Performing Artist
- Producers - Payout points- PRO - CAE, SRCO, ISRC
- Spotify -Interactive
- Internet Radio - Non Interactive
- Pandora - Non Interactive
- Youtube - Interactive
- Fm Radio - Non Interactive
- UBE - 10 Seconds to get Adsense
- Your Song used in Commercial - Payout PRO
- Song used in Pandora -Payout SE
- Song used on Radio -Payout BDS
- Song used on YouTube - Payout -Aggregator
- Song used in video games - Payout Harry Fox Agency -Aggregator
- Song used in Licensing Deal -Pay Out Music Reports

- Songwriter - Pay Out PRO

The payout is different when it comes to these platforms such as radio, Apple, Pandora, Apple, iTunes, spottily, in concert and in the mall. So just know that BMI is not paying or collecting royalties for your song streaming on online radio. BMI does not cover digital non interactives. Your songs have to be submitted to BMI so it tracks airplay and how many times it was played. If your song is not in an aggregator you're not collecting on behalf of HFA, you're only being Adsense payout, no recorded royalties. If your song is on Pandora and you aren't the MOC and SRCO, you're only collecting performing artists. If you have SoundScan and no UPCs, 30 days of no profit is marked. If you have your song on Spotify and you don't own full monetizations through aggregators, you're only getting 16 cents vs spin vs 96 cents. If you have your song on the radio, the only person collecting is CAE and the composer. Having BMI, SOUNDEXCHANGE and SOUNDSCAN is one thing but how to use them and why is a whole other ball game. So my question to you is;

do you have what it takes to be an independent artist? I am sure you do but now, are you willing to do what it takes? Well, the rest is up to you. Good luck, grind and get your hustle.

I wish you the best at everything, now go out there and be great

Yours truly Ladi Miz

www.ingramcontent.com/pod-product-compliance
Lightning Source LLC
Chambersburg PA
CBHW071731040426
42446CB00011B/2311